Sports Fun!

Basketball

by Christina Leaf

BLASTOFF! Beginners

BELLWETHER MEDIA
MINNEAPOLIS, MN

Blastoff! Beginners are developed by literacy experts and educators to meet the needs of early readers. These engaging informational texts support young children as they begin reading about their world. Through simple language and high frequency words paired with crisp, colorful photos, Blastoff! Beginners launch young readers into the universe of independent reading.

Sight Words in This Book

a	long	they	we
each	more	this	with
has	on	three	
into	people	time	
is	play	to	
it	the	two	

This edition first published in 2024 by Bellwether Media, Inc.

No part of this publication may be reproduced in whole or in part without written permission of the publisher. For information regarding permission, write to Bellwether Media, Inc., Attention: Permissions Department, 6012 Blue Circle Drive, Minnetonka, MN 55343.

Library of Congress Cataloging-in-Publication Data

Names: Leaf, Christina, author.
Title: Basketball / by Christina Leaf.
Description: Minneapolis, MN : Bellwether Media, Inc., 2024. | Series: Sports fun! | Includes bibliographical references and index. | Audience: Ages 4-7 | Audience: Grades K-1
Identifiers: LCCN 2023004980 (print) | LCCN 2023004981 (ebook) | ISBN 9798886873917 (library binding) | ISBN 9798886875799 (ebook)
Subjects: LCSH: Basketball--Juvenile literature.
Classification: LCC GV885.1 .L39 2024 (print) | LCC GV885.1 (ebook) | DDC 796.323--dc23/eng/20230202
LC record available at https://lccn.loc.gov/2023004980
LC ebook record available at https://lccn.loc.gov/2023004981

Text copyright © 2024 by Bellwether Media, Inc. BLASTOFF! BEGINNERS and associated logos are trademarks and/or registered trademarks of Bellwether Media, Inc.

Editor: Rebecca Sabelko   Designer: Jeffrey Kollock

Printed in the United States of America, North Mankato, MN.

Table of Contents

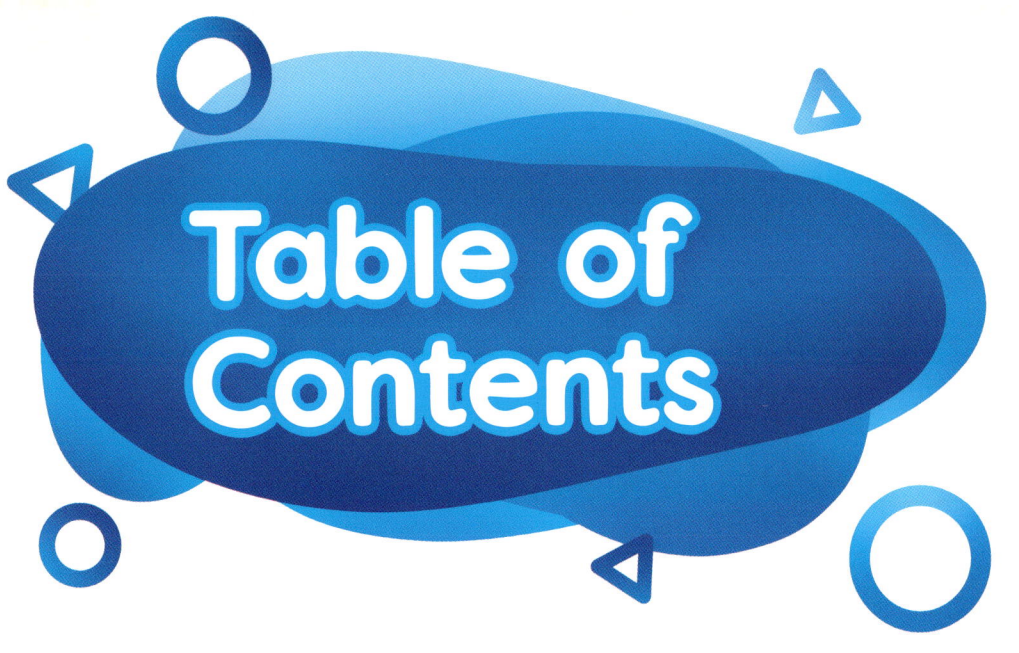

Game Time!	4
What Is Basketball?	6
Let's Play!	10
Basketball Facts	22
Glossary	23
To Learn More	24
Index	24

Game Time!

We head to the **court**. It is time to play basketball!

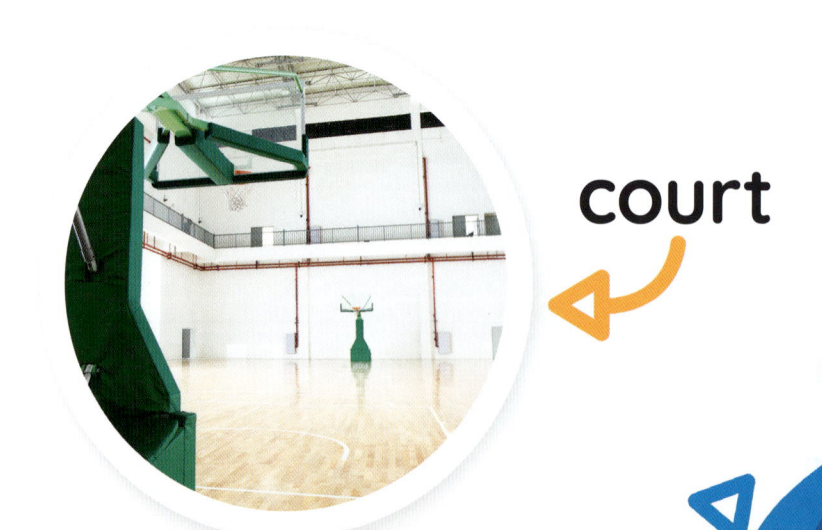

court

5

What Is Basketball?

Basketball is a team sport. People play on a court.

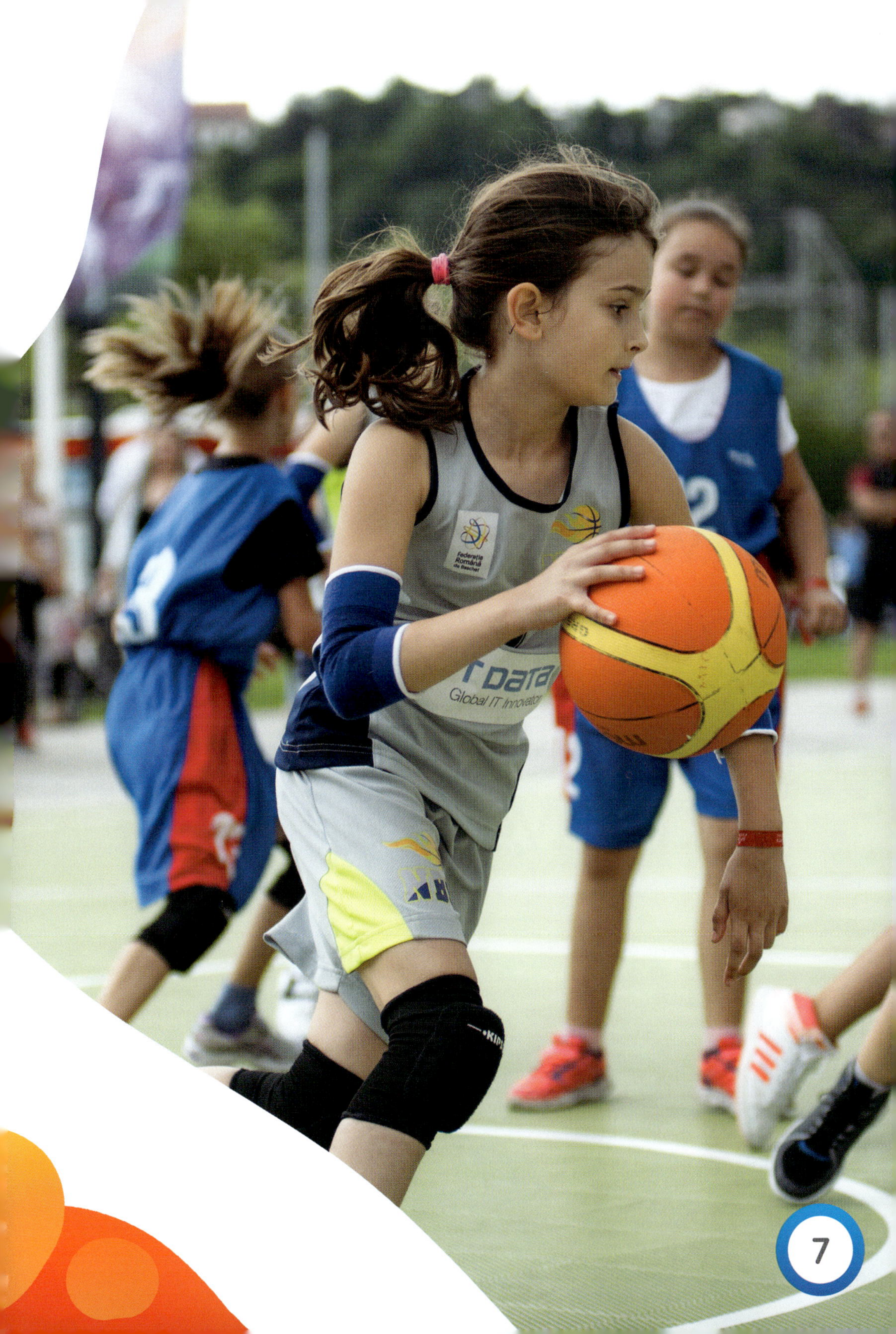
Global IT Innovator

Two teams
play a game.
Each team
has five players.

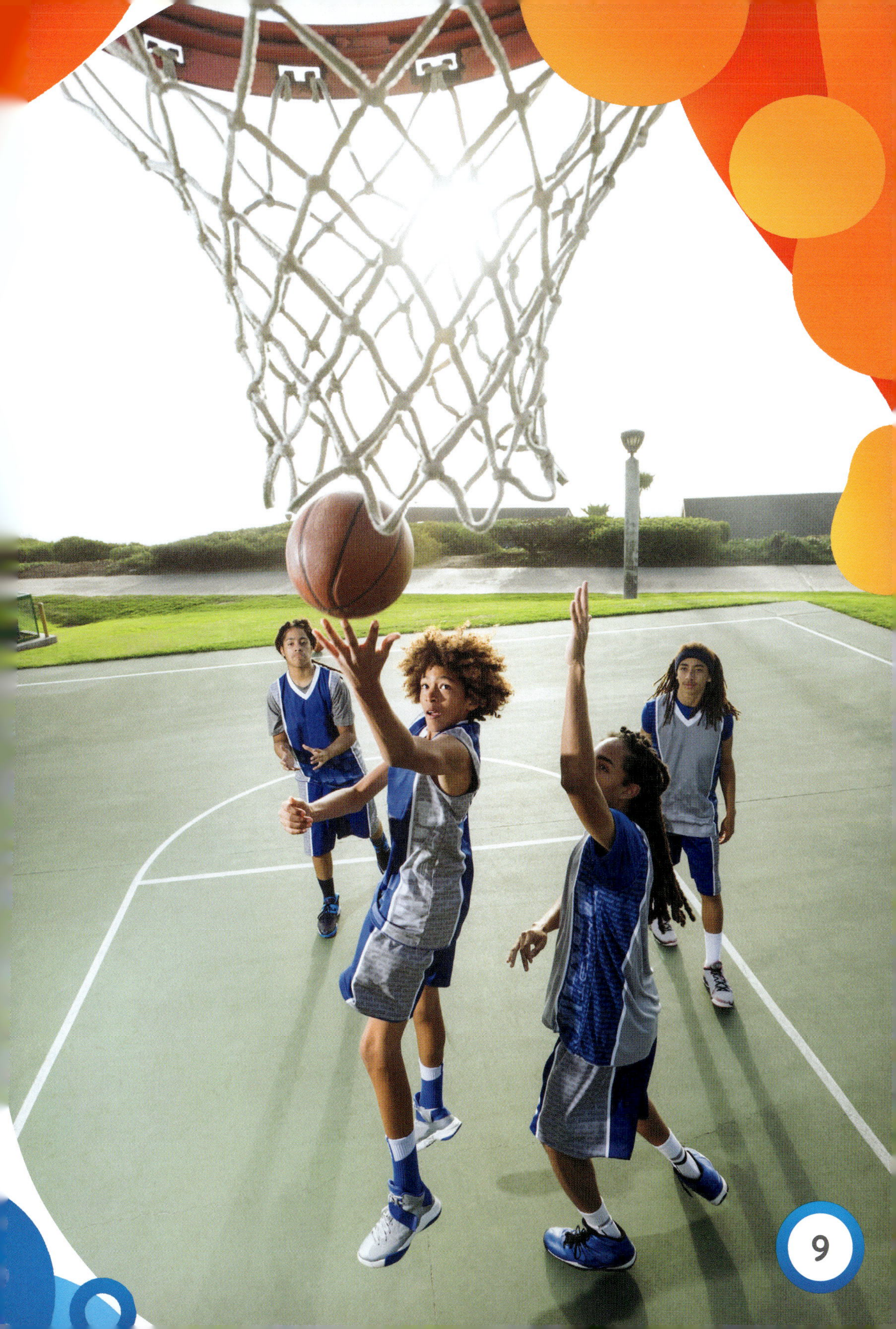

Let's Play!

Players **dribble** the basketball. They move with it.

dribble

Players pass the ball. They throw it to teammates.

passing

13

Players try to score. They shoot the ball into the **hoop**.

hoop

shooting

Most shots score two points.

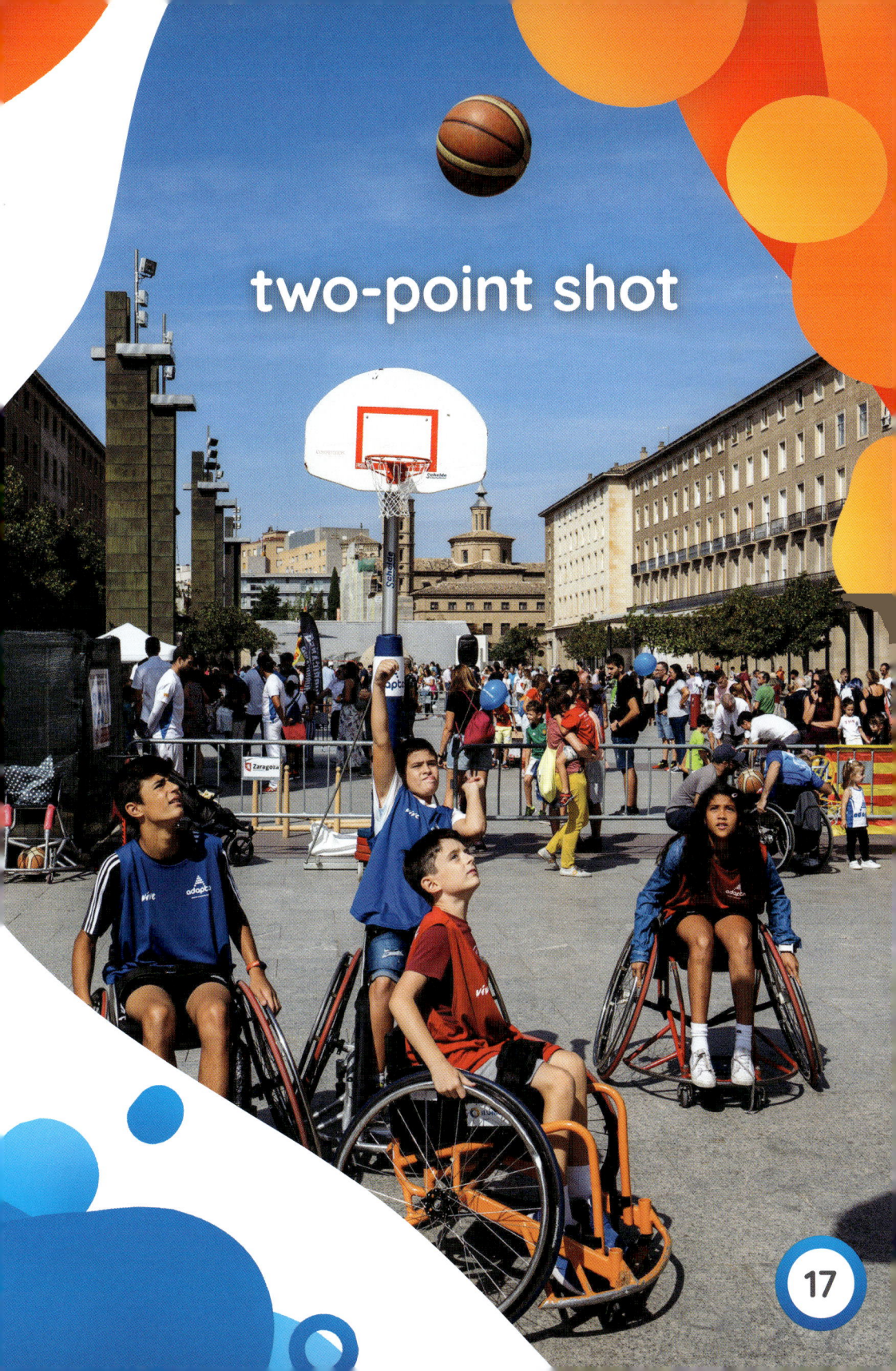

two-point shot

Long shots score three points!

three-point shot

The game is over. This team scored more points. They win!

21

Basketball Facts

Playing Basketball

basketball

hoop

court

Basketball Moves

dribble    pass    shoot

Glossary

court

a place where people play basketball

dribble

to bounce a basketball on the floor or ground

hoop

a tall ring players shoot basketballs into

To Learn More

ON THE WEB

FACTSURFER

Factsurfer.com gives you a safe, fun way to find more information.

1. Go to www.factsurfer.com.

2. Enter "basketball" into the search box and click 🔍.

3. Select your book cover to see a list of related content.

Index

ball, 10, 12, 14
court, 4, 6
dribble, 10, 11
game, 8, 20
hoop, 14, 15
pass, 12, 13
play, 4, 6, 8
players, 8, 10, 12, 14

points, 16, 17, 18, 19, 20
score, 14, 16, 18, 20
shoot, 14, 15
shot, 16, 17, 18, 19
team, 6, 8, 20
teammates, 12

win, 20

The images in this book are reproduced through the courtesy of: FabrikaSimf, front cover; Mike Flippo, front cover; Tom Saga, p. 3; hxdbzxy, pp. 4, 23 (court); Sergey Novikov, p. 5; salajean, p. 7; Erik Isakson, p. 9; Dmytro Zinkevych, p. 11; FatCamera, p. 13; Viacheslav Nikolaenko, p. 15; Nano Calvo/ Alamy, p. 17; Ljupco Smokovski, p. 18; South_agency, pp. 19, 22 (pass); HRUAN, p. 21; RodfaiStudio, p. 22 (playing basketball); Sergey Ryzhov, p. 22 (dribble); Lopolo, pp. 22 (shoot), 23 (dribble); clkgtr37, p. 23 (hoop).

24